GOD
Is Always Watching
Over You

GOD
Is Always Watching Over You

Inspiring Words About
God's Constant Presence
in Our Lives

Edited by Angela Joshi

Blue Mountain Press™
Boulder, Colorado

We gratefully acknowledge the permission granted by the following authors, publishers, and authors' representatives to reprint poems or excerpts from their publications.

Karen Taylor-Good for "God Is in Charge." Copyright © 2009 by Karen Taylor-Good. All rights reserved.

Doubleday, a division of Random House, Inc., for "Through years of study, prayer, and…" from POWERFUL INSPIRATIONS: EIGHT LESSONS THAT WILL CHANGE YOUR LIFE by Kathy Ireland and Laura Morton. Copyright © 2002 by Kathy Ireland WorldWide, Inc. All rights reserved.

Linda E. Knight for "He Will Be Your Shelter," "He Will Be with You Through Every Storm Life Brings Your Way," "One Day at a Time," and "He Will Always See You Through." Copyright © 2011 by Linda E. Knight. All rights reserved.

Random House, Inc., for "One day the teacher…" and "My faith is tested many times…" from WOULDN'T TAKE NOTHING FOR MY JOURNEY NOW by Maya Angelou. Copyright © 1993 by Maya Angelou. All rights reserved.

Broadway Books, a division of Random House, Inc., for "Some people have never seen…" from MOSAIC: PIECES OF MY LIFE SO FAR by Amy Grant. Copyright © 2007 by Amy Grant. All rights reserved. And for "Faith is a gateway to happiness…" and "I believe God will always answer…" from MARY LOU RETTON'S GATEWAYS TO HAPPINESS by Mary Lou Retton. Copyright © 2000 by MLR Entertainment, Inc. All rights reserved. And for "The midnight hour is a difficult period…" from HARD QUESTIONS, HEART ANSWERS by The Reverend Bernice A. King. Copyright © 1996 by Bernice A. King. All rights reserved.

Acknowledgments are continued on page 92.

Library of Congress Control Number: 2010912898
ISBN: 978-1-68088-251-3 (previously ISBN: 978-1-59842-596-3)

Printed in China.
Second printing of this edition: 2019

✪ This book is printed on recycled paper.

This book is printed on paper that has been specially produced to be acid free (neutral pH) and contains no groundwood or unbleached pulp. It conforms with the requirements of the American National Standards Institute, Inc., so as to ensure that this book will last and be enjoyed by future generations.

Blue Mountain Arts, Inc.
P.O. Box 4549, Boulder, Colorado 80306

Contents

God Is Always Watching Over You

When life overwhelms you
and you feel like you can't
   carry on,
hold out your hand to God.
He will give you strength
and walk beside you
when you think you can't
walk another step.

God will carry you
through life's trials;
He will help you make it
   through this day
and all those to come.
And He is always watching over you.

— Barbara J. Hall

God Has a Plan for You

Knowing God has a plan for your life is very important. When things happen that are out of your control, it can be very discouraging. It's easy to become frustrated, to feel afraid, and to question what the future holds. Putting your faith in God's plan allows you to trust that the events in your life are meant to be. It helps you to make choices that must be made and realize things are not really out of control — they are under His control.

There is a peace that can be found knowing that His plan is playing out in your life. When things are confusing for you, remember that God is in control and He loves you. Trust Him and His plans.

— Rick Norman

You are not alone and you never will be. God is with you every step of the way. Where the path leads, He is lighting lamps to guide you.

And if you ever do feel for a second that He is not right there beside you, it is only because He has gone ahead for a moment or two to build a bridge that will keep you safe from harm and that will lead you on toward the light shining through.

— Alin Austin

Follow the Beautiful Trail
Wherever He Leads You

Be open to what each day asks of you
and welcome what it may hold,
knowing the desires of your heart
   are in God's hands.
No matter where life leads,
He goes with you step by step
with open arms and heart;
trust Him on your journey.
He is the maker of every dream
and the keeper of all His promises;
share in the joy of celebrating
   what He's given you.
Find joy in every opportunity
to live out His purpose for you,
and know your efforts have meaning.
Accept any detours as part of His plan.
Keep your eyes on God,
and you'll never lose your way.

— Linda E. Knight

God Is in Charge

Life can sometimes feel
like you're out there alone
kind of lost in space — directionless.
Just remember
nothing could be further from the truth.

As a precious child of God
you are part of a master plan,
and even if you can't quite figure out
what your part is,
that's okay.

You can take a deep breath,
truly relax,
and know that all is well
because God is in charge.

— Karen Taylor-Good

Through years of study, prayer, and practical experience, I now understand that I truly want God to be in charge of all things, because He has a greater sense of the "big picture" than I ever could understand. I recognize that sometimes His path isn't the path I'd choose or the easiest road to travel, but it is always the path I need to be on in order to grow and fully enrich my life and the lives of those around me.

I am a bit of a control freak, so asking that God's will be done over my own is, in itself, a daily challenge for me. When I give up that control and accept that He is truly in charge of all things, I am at peace. I trust Him even though I know it doesn't always mean that everything is going to be easy. Life is tough, and you have to be, too. Every day we live is filled with uncertainty. As people of God, we don't know what tomorrow holds, but we know who holds tomorrow. God can make the impossible possible.

〜 Kathy Ireland

He Will Be Your Shelter

In the shelter of God's love,
there is comfort
for all of life's ups and downs.
In the hollow of His heart,
there's a place only you can fill.
In God's time, you will find new dreams,
new growth taking place.
In waiting for Him to come,
you'll find He's already here.
In every dream and every dawn,
touch the prayers urging you to keep trying.
In every concern,
feel the caring belief for a better day.
In every trial, there are lessons
your heart can learn.

May God give each day new meaning
and time give each dream new wings.
May God scatter your cares to the wind
as He carries you close to His heart.

~~~ Linda E. Knight

You Are Never Without God's Love

Knowing God loves us — at all times and without conditions — gives us strength, protection, hope, and peace. With God's love, we can achieve amazing things.

— April Weston

One day the teacher... asked that I read from *Lessons in Truth*, a section which ended with these words: "God loves me." I read the piece and closed the book, and the teacher said, "Read it again." I pointedly opened the book, and I sarcastically read, "God loves me." He said, "Again." After about the seventh repetition I began to sense that there might be truth in the statement, that there was a possibility that God really did love me. Me, Maya Angelou. I suddenly began to cry at the grandness of it all. I knew that if God loved me, then I could do wonderful things, I could try great things, learn anything, achieve anything. For what could stand against me with God, since one person, any person with God, constitutes the majority?

— Maya Angelou

Some people have never seen an ocean.
That doesn't change the ocean. It is
constant and powerful, and like the love
of God, whether we're immersed in it,
standing on the shore, or a thousand
miles away, it remains.

~ Amy Grant

My every thought, my every action, is a moment in
which divine support comes to me. I am never alone,
never an exile, never a stranger from the heart of God.
The heart of God holds me within its bountiful soil. I
blossom there, rooted in faith, fed by the nutrients of
divine love.

~ Julia Cameron

There's nothing as strong, as dependable,
   or as accepting —
and nothing that can heal as completely —
   as God's love.
You don't need to feel it
   to take advantage of it;
you just need to believe in it, embrace it,
   share it,
and allow it to guide your every thought
   and action.
The love of God is
   the greatest power of all,
and it's right inside of you.

— Barbara Cage

God Is in Everything Around You

Look at the sky,
and in its vastness
see the love God has for you.
Feel the wind,
and recognize God's touch.

Be aware of the gifts God has given you
every time you feel the connection
you share with family and friends.
Know that He placed them
in your life to fill it
with love you can touch.

Understand that the harder times
are just the uphill parts
of the path God has laid for you,
and if you follow the way faithfully,
He will lead you on
to places of peace and joy.

God surrounds us all the time.
He is in the bad things,
as He is in the good things.
Always strive to recognize God
in everything around you.

— Selina Maybury

With Each Sunrise, God Gives You a New Beginning

One of God's greatest gifts
is the chance to be born again
each day...

Beginning with every sunrise,
you can let go of the past
and any regrets, mistakes,
   or sorrows it may have held.
You can look ahead and see
   where you'd like to go,
secure in the knowledge that
God enables you to leave
   any emotional baggage
where it belongs — in the past.
You can choose to leave
   yesterday behind
and start over again today —
to be whoever and whatever
   you dream of being.
Know that with God's help
and His constant, loving attention,
you can achieve anything...
   beginning today.

               — Edmund O'Neill

A Morning Prayer to Fill Your Day with Peace and Joy

"As I stand on the edge of this day,
grant me the strength I need
    to move forward on this journey
        with grace.
Grant me the courage to travel
    with compassion as my companion
        through each hour,
the humor to lighten each moment
    and bring light and laughter
        to others I meet,
and the smiles to scatter along the path
    that stretches before me.

Grant me the wisdom to recognize stones
　　on my path and to be able to
　　　distinguish between
those I can move, those I can step over,
　　and those I need to leave alone.
Grant me the calmness to accept that
　　I don't always have to be right,
to face difficulties with serenity,
　　and to find peace within myself.
Grant me the skills and confidence
　　to face whatever challenges and joys
　　　this day brings,
and grant me the capacity to relish
　　every moment."
　　　　　　　～ Angela M. Churm

God Is
Always Listening

In your joyous moments,
He basks in your praise, thanks,
    and laughter.
When circumstances seem unjust,
    He hears your pleas.
In your times of meditative contemplation,
    He listens and inspires.
When life has dealt a low blow
and grief is your constant companion,
your cries wrench His heart.

And in those times when you cannot speak,
even then God hears your voice.

— Cindy B. Stevens

He Will Be with You Through All of Life's Storms

From time to time, when we least expect it, life changes course and worry washes over us like waves on a storm-tossed beach. Rough times happen. Good people suffer. Questions arise.

We may not be able to see or know or sense how everything will turn out — or even why it happened. But we can know that God is with us at each turn, on every journey.

Beyond every storm, God has something beautiful for you that is as precious as your heart and as special as you are — something as extraordinary as a rainbow after the rain.

Blue skies will come. Hope will dawn. God is as near to you in the storm as He is in the sunshine. Cherish the good memories. Put the bad ones behind you. Hope is as near as a prayer. Embrace His promises. Let Him shoulder your cares. Remember that you are never alone. Entrust your tomorrows to God.

Fair winds will blow once again. Smooth paths will follow. Calm waters will comfort you. Find peace in knowing that you are safe in His care… for God will always see you through anything.

⮬ Linda E. Knight

The Power of Faith

Faith
is trusting and
believing in a power
we can neither
see nor touch.
It's a feeling
born deep within
our hearts
that keeps us
holding on
even when we feel
all our strength
is gone.
It is a promise of hope
that whispers, "You'll be okay..."
even through the darkest times.

Faith
fills us with power
we could never
find on our own.
It is a bridge…
between your heart
and God.

— Jason Blume

Faith is a gateway to happiness that remains permanently accessible to each of us, wherever we are, no matter our circumstances. Like the lighthouse perched on rocky cliffs that steers lonely ships safely back to shore, faith can guide us to make better choices, become better individuals, and find our way to true happiness. Faith allows us to have a deep, personal relationship with our Creator and to explore the intricacies of our own souls. It is an unending supply of joy and sustenance that can help us through our darkest moments and open the door to lasting peace and fulfillment.

— Mary Lou Retton

Faith strips the mask from the world and reveals God in everything. It makes nothing impossible and renders meaningless such words as anxiety, danger, and fear, so that the believer goes through life calmly and peacefully, with profound joy — like a child hand in hand with his mother.

— Charles de Foucauld

The reason birds fly, and we can't, is simply that they have perfect faith, for to have perfect faith is to have wings.

~ Sir James M. Barrie

My faith is tested many times every day, and more times than I'd like to confess, I'm unable to keep the banner of faith aloft. If a promise is not kept, or if a secret is betrayed, or if I experience long-lasting pain, I begin to doubt God and God's love. I fall so miserably into the chasm of disbelief that I cry out in despair. Then the Spirit lifts me up again, and once more I am secured in faith. I don't know how that happens, save when I cry out earnestly I am answered immediately and am returned to faithfulness. I am once again filled with Spirit and firmly planted on solid ground.

~ Maya Angelou

Remember that you are a part
    of a limitless love
and you will find strength
    you never imagined.

The combination of your faith
    and God's power
can achieve things beyond
    your wildest dreams.

Allow His love into your soul,
and let Him guide you along the path
you were always meant to follow.

Trust that things will turn out
as they were meant to be.
God has brought you this far,
and He will always be
    close by your side.

— Jason Blume

God Will Be Your Strength in Tough Times

God allows us to experience the low points of life in order to teach us lessons we could not learn in any other way.

~~ C. S. Lewis

The midnight hour is a difficult period in a person's life....

No matter what midnight hour you're faced with, God can give you strength to live with it. Always remember that when you pray, God is working on your behalf. No matter what the midnight situation is, if you stay armed with prayer, God has a prescription for you. He will either remove it or give you the necessary strength to live through it. Therefore, rest in the knowledge that none of your prayers go unnoticed because through prayer you invoke God's power to work in your life.

~~ The Reverend Bernice A. King

I was taught by a great teacher at one time that whenever you're having a problem, whenever you're struggling with anything in your life, whenever your mind is filled with the struggles of your life, the way to make that problem go away, in that instant, is to think of God, rather than the problem that you're focused on.

❧ Wayne Dyer

I wish I'd known that God would give me all the strength and faith I needed to go through some of my own tough times.... Perhaps I wouldn't have been so afraid.

❧ Maria Shriver

He Is Never Far Away

When we are hurting
God doesn't stay on high —
He brings His majesty to earth
on the wings of love.
When we encounter trials and tribulations,
it is God who will help us face whatever
    is happening in our hearts.
He pours His peace into the moments,
holds our hands and calms our fears.
He walks with us and talks with us
    along the way.
When we need the ultimate in compassion —
the greatest caring, true concern —
it is God's love that wipes each tear away
and brings tomorrow's hope.

God isn't far away...
    He's always by your side.

— Barbara J. Hall

Life Can Be as Simple as a Prayer

Too often discouragement, unhappiness,
    and stress
take a toll on our lives and rob us
    of the joy we're entitled to.
It's at those times that we must not take
    the power of prayer for granted;
we should stop what we're doing
    and focus on God.
In stressful times, we should consciously
    back off from the situation
and take a moment to reflect on what's
    really important.
A conversation with God has a way
    of putting things in perspective.
He often helps us change our attitude,
    find a solution, or see the humor.

God shows us what our talents
     and gifts are
and how to put them to use for our
     success and peace of mind.
God reminds us that mistakes and failures
     are okay;
He helps us learn from them and gives us
     the confidence to go on.
Life can be tough with all its challenges
     and problems —
we get tired and fed up, and sometimes
     we feel overwhelmed —
but it really isn't all that difficult
     when you have God...
That's when life is as simple
     as a prayer.
                              ～ Barbara Cage

Prayer is a way that our hearts
can communicate in faith,
a way that we can ask questions
and receive answers, ·
a way that we can openly express
our feelings and concerns.
Prayer is a wonderful source of
strength for a person,
and prayers can become even
stronger when we turn to each
other for support in prayer.
Lean on prayer to help you through
difficult times,
and know with certainty what the
power of prayer can do.

— Susan Hickman Sater

When it seems hardest
to pray, pray hardest.

~~ Hugh Black

Eyes raised toward heaven are always beautiful.

~~ Joseph Joubert

God Will Answer Your Prayers

The essential thing is not what we say but what God says to us and through us. In that silence, He will listen to us; there He will speak to our soul, and there we will hear His voice.

— Mother Teresa

If prayer is you talking to God, then intuition is God talking to you.

— Wayne Dyer

Have you heard God's voice? At the same time you are searching for God, He is speaking to you.

— Billy Graham

I believe God will always answer your questions and He will also answer your prayers, but many people think that the answers are always "yes." And that's not the case. Sometimes the answer has to be "no." It may not be what we want to hear, but if that's the answer God gives, we have to accept His wisdom. I don't believe for a moment that sometimes God doesn't hear me or that He says, "I'm not going to answer Mary Lou on this one." When I was a child, I sometimes wondered, as we all do, why God "didn't answer." Wasn't I praying the right way? Hadn't I been as good a girl as I could possibly be? Had He stopped loving me? As I matured in my faith, I came to see that all the times I thought God wasn't listening, He was actually saying "No," or "Not now, you'll have to wait."

➳ Mary Lou Retton

Let God Help

He has helped so many through
   so much.
And He will be there for you
   in your most personal moments
   and through all the times of your life,
      whether they are troubled
         or triumphant.

Take comfort in that thought.
Hold it inside you
   this day and all the days
      of your life.
                              — Alin Austin

One Day at a Time

God speaks to us through our lives,
through the smiles and the shadows,
through the times, ever changing.

God calls to us on our journeys,
    putting the broken pieces
        back together again.

God comforts us in our tears
    until life, at its worst,
        becomes something better.

God strengthens us in our weakness
    until His power is all that we feel.

God opens the door to our dreams
and gives us each day as a gift.

God feels the depth and the texture
of all our longings within.

God rejoices in our hope and our promise
as a mother rejoices over her child.

God sees only the best in the shadows
of what's yet to be.

God speaks to us through our lives,
one day and one step at a time.

— Linda E. Knight

God's Blessings
Are Ours to Cherish

There is so much to be thankful for
in this world —
the love of our family,
a warm home, good friends,
our health and happiness,
the beauty that surrounds us.

Yet when things aren't going our way,
when sorrow enters our lives
or dreams seem out of reach,
we too quickly forget how fortunate
we really are.

When difficulties occur,
we must learn to rise above the
feelings of sadness and despair.
We must accept the wisdom of God's plan
and go on with our lives,
grateful for His many blessings,
secure in His love.

— Anna Marie Edwards

In Difficult Times, Know That He Will Hold You in His Arms

It's only a matter of time before the storms in your life subside. The clouds will pass, and the sun will show its face. The rain that has fallen will remind you of the tears you've shed. There will come a respite and a calm.

Through it all, you will feel a presence by your side. You will sense a light shining inside the dark corners of your heart. That light will uplift and guide you away from the shadows into the glorious warmth of day.

God will hold you in His arms. He will be the
rainbow at the end of your storms.

Though you may feel alone, He will hold you
in His heart. He will steady your arm when
you stumble. He will be your eyes when you
can't see.

The storm will subside. Hope will rise to take
its place, and you will break through to the
light — by the grace of God.

— Josie Willis

God Never Gives Up,
and Neither Should You

When you're hurt and confused
and things are hard to accept
    or understand,
give them to God
and He will give you peace and faith.

When you've been treated rudely
    or unfairly
and hatred and anger rule your soul,
talk to God about it
and He will give you a forgiving,
    calm spirit.

When you're overwhelmed with
    too much to do
and stressed out because of lack of time,
let God guide you
and He will show you where your
    priorities should be.

When you're feeling down and discouraged
and you aren't living up to your
    own dreams and expectations,
let God be your partner
and He will give you power and strength.

When things get tough and you want
    to give up,
don't…
and God won't either.

              — Barbara Cage

God Knows...

When you are tired
and discouraged from
fruitless efforts...
God knows how hard
you have tried.
When you've cried so long
and your heart is in anguish...
God has counted your tears.
If you feel that your life
is on hold
and time has passed you by...
God is waiting with you.
When you're lonely
and your friends are too busy
even for a phone call...
God is by your side.
When you think you've tried everything
and don't know where to turn...
God has a solution.
When nothing makes sense
and you are confused
or frustrated...
God has the answer.

If suddenly your outlook is brighter
and you find traces of hope...
God has whispered to you.
When things are going well
and you have much to be
thankful for...
God has blessed you.
When something joyful happens
and you are filled with awe...
God has smiled on you.
When you have a purpose to fulfill
and a dream to follow...
God has opened your eyes
and called you by name.
Remember that wherever you are
or whatever you're facing...
God knows.

                   — Kelly D. Williams

May You Find Answers to the Prayers That You Pray

May you find the gold at the end of your rainbow.
May you chase every dark cloud away.
May you find a way to move all your mountains.
May you find answers to the prayers that you pray.

Looking back, you see only what was fact,
    what was true.
Looking ahead, you see your future and
    you dream of a way.
As you gather up all your wishes and hide them
    in your heart,
may you find answers to the prayers that you pray.

If you keep trying to reach it, but your goal
    is elusive,
if you don't know whether to move on or to stay,
I wish you starships to guide you and
    angels to hold you.
May you find answers to the prayers that you pray.

                                    ━ Donna Fargo

God's Light Will Inspire Your Heart

This light can awaken dreams.
It creates beauty previously unimagined,
fulfills promises and provides peace,
teaches wisdom and strengthens the weak.

This light can change anything.
It turns the hardest heart to tears,
transforms jealousy into gentleness,
replaces resentment with fulfillment.

This light teaches forgiveness and patience.
It comforts pain and soothes anger,
believes in miracles and encourages hope,
survives defeat and continues forever.

This light shines on —
bright as the stars in heaven.
It is a flame in the darkness of defeat,
a flicker of hope that never ends,
a spark to fulfill God's design for our lives.

When love sparks a heart and
inspires tenderness and hope,
it is always spiritual —
a sign of God's light inside us.

Always reach toward the light,
and God will guide you from the inside.
Simply follow the light,
and you will find the key you need
to discover your inner beauty
and fulfill God's plan for you.

— Regina Hill

Some of the best advice
a person can share with someone
they care about is this...

"God will be there for you."

If you need to lean on someone,
    there is no greater strength.
If you need to move away from
    difficulty and toward resolve,
    there is no greater direction to go.
If you wish to walk with happiness,
    there is no greater traveling companion.

Follow your heart when it tells you to believe,
because there is no end to the blessings
    you can receive.

"God will be there for you."

━ Alin Austin

"Please Watch Over Someone I Care About"

Oh, Lord, please watch over someone I care so much about. Please do it for them… and for me.

Please help to make this day and all that follow a time of comfort and understanding.

Please help the light of serenity shine in through an open door, warming the heart and encouraging the soul of somebody who lovingly needs to know that they are dearly thought of and cared for and that someone is always there for them.

Please help to chase away any clouds and lessen any troubles in this day.

Please help to provide the reassurance that hope, blessings, and a world of beautiful things are always there if we just take the time to see.

Please help us learn that life goes on and the difficulties that inevitably come to everyone turn into insurmountable concerns only if we let them.

Please help us realize that problems can only impact us to the extent that we give them power over our hearts and minds.

Please empower us with patience, faith, and love.

Please help us to choose the path we walk instead of letting it choose us.

Please let it take us to the brighter day that is always there, even though it is not always seen.

Please help us to be wiser than our worries, stronger than any situation that can come our way, and steadily assured of our beliefs.

Please help us reach the goals that wait for us on the horizons that encourage us.

Please enfold us within each new sunset and inspire us with each new dawn.

Please help someone who is so deserving of every goodness and kindness life can bring.

Please, Lord, help to show the way.

— Douglas Pagels

God Gave Us One Another

God gave us the seasons —
    each with its own beauty and reason,
      each meant to bring us a blessing,
        a joy, and a feeling of love.
God gave us the sunshine, the rain,
    and the beauty and freedom of nature
to teach us the wisdom of gentle acceptance.

God gave us miracles
in our hearts and lives,
little things that happen
to remind us we're alive.
God gave us the ability
to face each new day
with courage, wisdom,
and a smile from knowing
that whatever sorrow or pain we face,
He abides with us
securely in our hearts.
Most of all, God gave us one another
to teach us about love
and guide us through this world,
always available to help us forward
toward a greater understanding
and a greater sharing and giving
of love.
— Regina Hill

Have Faith!

When you dream, believe in
your ability to fulfill your wishes.
Believe — have faith —
and you will exceed your own expectations.

When you work, treat each task as a gift
and a chance to demonstrate your strengths.
Believe — have faith —
and each duty will bring a sense of purpose.

When you regret some past mistake or failure,
don't allow pessimism to influence you.
Believe — have faith —
and know that your past is gone.
Tomorrow you'll have a second chance.

When you hurt and no one seems to understand,
reach into your heart and be your own comfort.
You have the strength within.
Believe — have faith —
and your pain will pass into yesterday.

When you love, love with all your heart and soul.
Give without limit or expectation.
Believe — have faith —
and love will inspire your entire life.

Believe — have faith —
and remember that you are God's child…
and whatever He designs is perfect.

— Regina Hill

How Much Does God Love You?

Do you ever look up to see the stars at night?
Have you tried to count them all
or imagine their number,
feeling small and insignificant
and overwhelmed at the sight?

Do you ever try to picture
the hand that put each star in its place,
that knows their number,
and — more importantly —
knows that you are looking up
to see the vastness of His universe?
He sees your face, hears your thoughts,
and reads your heart.

God loves you more than
    all the stars in heaven.
There's an endless amount of love
    that He is always sending you,
and His love is there to cover
    every moment of your life.

— Barbara J. Hall

Everything That Touches Your Heart Is a Gift from God

A friend who takes the time
   to stop and chat.
A smile.
A hand on your shoulder in a time of need.
An unspoken prayer
answered in a most uncommon way.
The best gift of all is to understand
that you are never alone...
because when you touch a flower,
catch that first raindrop on your fingertips,
or see the wonder of a child,
you see God.

It is the reality and profound blessing
   of knowing
that in an infinite number of ways...
God is always with you.

— Linda Hersey

God isn't far away.
He is the light of this day.
He is the sky above you,
the earth beneath you,
and the life of every living thing.

He is in every smile,
in every thought that gives you hope,
in every tear that waters your soul,
and in every moment you can't
face alone.

He's the love on your loved one's face.
He's in the friends along the way —
in strangers you have yet to meet
and blessings you have yet to receive.

He's in every good thing
that touches you.
He is in every step you make
and every breath you take.
He is never far away.

— Nancye Sims

Anything Is Possible
Because of Him

It is God who enables you
to smile in spite of tears;
to carry on when you feel like giving in;
to pray when you're at a loss for words;
to love even though your heart has been
    broken time and time again;
to sit calmly when you feel like throwing
    your hands up in frustration;
to be understanding when nothing
    seems to make sense;
to listen when you'd really rather not hear;
to share your feelings with others
    because sharing is necessary
        to ease the load.

Anything is possible
because God makes it so.

— Faye Sweeney

Expect a Miracle

Miracles can and do happen. They can come at any time. Even when things seem darkest, there is a miracle nearby.

God knows when things are getting you down and He needs to let you know how much He cares. That's when He gives you the miracle you've been looking for. In that moment, the clouds part and the sun will come through for you.

— Rodger Austin

Miracles come in moments.
Be ready and willing!

— Wayne Dyer

Keep believing in the here-and-now,
down-to-earth, everyday kind of miracles —
like the first star emerging in the evening sky,
the sun breaking through a storm,
and that amazing rainbow over your world.
Catch a glimpse of heaven in every person's face.
Keep believing in bright endings,
in giving more than you receive,
and in the overwhelming goodness of people.
See the miracle of each new day
as spectacular and unique
as the sunrise that brings it.

Miracles come wrapped in a stranger's smile,
in a kind word just when you need it most,
and, especially, in a friend's hug.
Everyday miracles are always happening.
Just open your eyes.
You may not have to see it to believe it,
but you may have to believe it to see it.

— Vickie M. Worsham

God Is Everywhere

A look around the world reminds us
that God is in control —
holding up each star,
sending sunshine down to earth,
bringing beauty into life.

One glance around the world can give
our hearts a peaceful feeling
of security in knowing that
God is watching over us.
He won't forget to let the rivers flow
or keep the flowers blooming
    in their fields.

He colors in the spaces of our lives
with moments to be thankful for
    and tender, loving care.
With His majestic touch, each night
    turns into day
as the sun wakes up the world again
    and time blesses us once more.

It's a wondrous thing to look at life
and realize
that the old, old story of God's love
continues on.
He's in control, and He keeps
all things beautiful for us.

— Barbara J. Hall

Look Out for the Angels in Your Life

The very presence of an angel is a communication. Even when an angel crosses our path in silence, God has said to us, "I am here. I am present in your life."

— Tobias Palmer

Angels are breaths of God.

— Lactantius

Angels... come as visions, voices, dreams, coincidences, and intuition, the whisper of knowledge at your ear They come as animals or other people, or as a wash of peace in an ailing heart. Sometimes a stranger may come up and give you just the information or assistance you need. Sometimes you yourself are used as an angel, for a moment, either knowingly or not, speaking words you did not know you knew.

But sometimes these beings come as angels, in the very form that artists show — as beings of light, both with and without wings.

— Sophy Burnham

Have you ever felt that inner tug
    or a silent voice of caution
    or an invisible hand leading you
        down some new path?
Has the light of an exciting new idea
    suddenly lit up in your mind,
        or has an inner sense of love made you
            rise up to help someone in need?
If you look closely
    you might just see
        an angel sitting on your shoulder.
This heavenly messenger is your own
    personal guardian sent to keep you safe
    and lead you down the steep paths of life.
Your angel will direct your steps
    and watch over you.
Don't worry. Don't give up.
    Just turn your head,
    and you will see your newest friend
        sitting on your shoulder...
    making sure everything is okay.

                                    ━━ Dan Lynch

May you always have an angel by your side ⚫
Watching out for you in all the things you do ⚫
Reminding you to keep believing in brighter
days ⚫ Finding ways for your wishes and dreams
to come true ⚫ Giving you hope that is as certain
as the sun ⚫ Giving you the strength of serenity
as your guide ⚫ May you always have love and
comfort and courage ⚫

May you always have an angel by your side ⚫
Someone there to catch you if you fall ⚫
Encouraging your dreams ⚫ Inspiring your
happiness ⚫ Holding your hand and helping you
through it all ⚫ In all of our days, our lives are
always changing ⚫ Tears come along as well as
smiles ⚫ Along the roads you travel, may the miles
be a thousand times more lovely than lonely ⚫

And may you always have an angel
by your side ⚫

— Douglas Pagels

May All These Wonderful Blessings Be Yours...

The Gift of Love

May you love and be loved by the people who mean the most to you. Allow love to give you a constant sense of balance and soulful and spiritual nourishment.

Good Health

May you be physically, mentally, and emotionally well, and may you have the wisdom and ability to maintain good health all the days of your life.

A Joyful Heart

May your attitude about life lead you to love others as well as yourself. May it help you deal with whatever you encounter in life: success, failure, pleasure, disappointment, and all the in-betweens.

The Loyalty of Family

May you have a supportive family... people to go home
to... people close to you who know where you came
from and where you are now... people who care about
you just as you care about them.

The Treasure of Friendship

May you have friends who enrich your life, want the
best for you, and support you the way you always do
for them.

Genuine Happiness

May you always have the freedom and opportunity to
express yourself creatively so you can be who you want
to be. When you need reassurance, may you turn your
fears into faith and your doubts into trust. Happiness
is your birthright. Claim it.

— Donna Fargo

God Will Take Care of You

Someone's watching over you
   with the greatest love.
Someone wants you to be
   happy, safe, and secure.
Someone considers you
   a wonderful individual
   and cares about your needs.
Someone's making blessings
   for your benefit right now —
like sunshine for those rainy days
and rainbows to remind you
   of the promise up ahead.

Someone's watching over you always...
   and He will take good care of you.

— Barbara J. Hall

He Will Always
See You Through

Like a star shining over you,
the special dreams God has for you
are always within your reach.
Life has so many wonderful things
in store for you;
set no limits on yourself.
God makes the impossible possible;
all it takes is a willing heart.
Let go of yesterday; let tomorrow in.
God gives you hope
to do the most difficult things
and courage to try again.

Your potential is unlimited;
open your eyes to the possibilities.
Trust in the One who gives you
strength to carry on,
and step into the future
knowing God is there with you.
Little reminders of Him
are all around you —
in every hug, smile, and prayer.
You can never go so far
that His love cannot reach you,
and it will always see you through.

~ Linda E. Knight

May You Always Feel God's Presence

May the paths you walk and the roads you travel take you to amazing places — places where you see the possibilities, where you discover what it's like when dreams come true, and where you come to understand the promise and the potential of all the wonderful qualities inside you.

May God's plan for you gradually unfold before your eyes, and — like guiding lights continually showing the way — may you find glimmers of hope and happiness shining every single day.

May the people in your life appreciate what it's like to be in the presence of someone as special as you are. You have the kind of gifts that are given to so few.

God has a plan for each of us... and may you know there is an especially wonderful one... for you.

— Alin Austin

Acknowledgments continued...

We gratefully acknowledge the permission granted by the following authors, publishers, and authors' representatives to reprint poems or excerpts from their publications.

Jeremy P. Tarcher, a division of Penguin Group (USA), Inc., for "My every thought..." from BLESSINGS: PRAYERS AND DECLARATIONS FOR A HEARTFUL LIFE by Julia Cameron. Copyright © 1998 by Julia Cameron. All rights reserved.

Barbara Cage for "There's nothing as strong...," "Life Can Be as Simple as a Prayer," "God Never Gives Up, and Neither Should You." Copyright © 2011 by Barbara Cage. All rights reserved.

Angela M. Churm for "A Morning Prayer to Fill Your Day with Peace and Joy." Copyright © 2011 by Angela M. Churm. All rights reserved.

Cindy B. Stevens for "God Is Always Listening." Copyright © 2002 by Cindy B. Stevens. All rights reserved.

Jason Blume for "Remember that you are a part...." and "The Power of Faith." Copyright © 2006, 2010 by Jason Blume. All rights reserved.

Hay House, Inc., Carlsbad, CA, for "I was taught by a great teacher" from GETTING IN THE GAP: MAKING CONSCIOUS CONTACT WITH GOD THROUGH MEDITATION by Wayne W. Dyer. Copyright © 2003 by Wayne W. Dyer. All rights reserved. And for "If prayer is you talking" from EVERYDAY WISDOM by Wayne W. Dyer. Copyright © 1993, 2005 by Wayne W. Dyer. All rights reserved.

Grand Central Publishing for "I wish I'd known that God..." from TEN THINGS I WISH I'D KNOWN BEFORE I WENT OUT INTO THE REAL WORLD by Maria Shriver. Copyright © 2000 by Maria Shriver. Reprinted by permission of Grand Central Publishing. All rights reserved.

Susan Hickman Sater for "Prayer is a way that...." Copyright © 2011 by Susan Hickman Sater. All rights reserved.

Word Publishing, a division of Thomas Nelson, Inc., Nashville, Tennessee, for "Have you heard God's voice?" from HOW TO BE BORN AGAIN by Billy Graham. Copyright © 1977, 1989 by Billy Graham. All rights reserved.

New World Library, Novato, CA, www.newworldlibrary.com, for "The essential thing is not..." from NO GREATER LOVE by Mother Teresa. Copyright © 1997, 2001 by New World Library. All rights reserved.

Josie Willis for "In Difficult Times, Know That He Will Hold You in His Arms." Copyright © 2011 by Josie Willis. All rights reserved.

PrimaDonna Entertainment Corp. for "May You Find Answers to the Prayers That You Pray" and "May All These Wonderful Blessings Be Yours..." by Donna Fargo. Copyright © 2002 by PrimaDonna Entertainment Corp. All rights reserved.

Regina Hill for "God's Light Will Inspire Your Heart" and "Have Faith!" Copyright © 2011 by Regina Hill. All rights reserved.

Barbara J. Hall for "How Much Does God Love You?" and "God Is Everywhere." Copyright © 2011 by Barbara J. Hall. All rights reserved.

Linda Hersey for "Everything That Touches Your Heart Is a Gift from God." Copyright © 2002 by Linda Hersey. All rights reserved.

Rodger Austin for "Miracles can and do happen." Copyright © 2011 by Rodger Austin. All rights reserved.

HarperCollins Publishers for "Miracles come in moments" from REAL MAGIC: CREATING MIRACLES IN EVERYDAY LIFE by Wayne W. Dyer. Copyright © 1992 by Wayne W. Dyer. All rights reserved. And for "The very presence of an angel..." from AN ANGEL IN MY HOUSE by Tobias Palmer. Copyright © 1994 by Winston Weathers. All rights reserved.

Vickie M. Worsham for "Keep believing in the here-and-now...." Copyright © 2011 by Vickie M. Worsham. All rights reserved.

Ballantine Books, a division of Random House, Inc., for "Angels... come as visions..." from ANGEL LETTERS by Sophy Burnham. Copyright © 1991 by Sophy Burnham. All rights reserved.

A careful effort has been made to trace the ownership of poems used in this anthology in order to obtain permission to reprint copyrighted materials and give proper credit to the copyright owners. If any error or omission has occurred, it is completely inadvertent, and we would like to make corrections in future editions provided that written notification is made to the publisher:

BLUE MOUNTAIN ARTS, INC., P.O. Box 4549, Boulder, Colorado 80306.